21ST
Century
Skills Library

GLOBAL PRODUCTS

COLAS

Kevin Cunningham

Cherry Lake Publishing
Ann Arbor, Michigan

663.62
Cunningham

Published in the United States of America by Cherry Lake Publishing
Ann Arbor, MI
www.cherrylakepublishing.com

Content Adviser: Edward Kolodziej, Director, Global Studies Program, University of
Illinois, Champaign, Illinois

Photo Credits: Cover and page 1, © Charles Jean Marc/Corbis Sygma; page 4, ©
Wolfgang Kaehler/Corbis; page 6, Photo courtesy of The Coca-Cola Company; page
13, © Noel Laura/Corbis Sygma; page 22, © Louie Psihoyos/Corbis; page 24, © Keith
Dannemiller/Corbis; page 27, © B.S.P.I./Corbis

Library of Congress Cataloging-in-Publication Data
Cunningham, Kevin.
 Global products. Colas / by Kevin Cunningham.
   p. cm.
 ISBN-13: 978-1-60279-025-4
 ISBN-10: 1-60279-025-6
 1. Carbonated beverages. 2. Cola drinks. I. Title. II. Title: Cola.
 TP630.C86 2008
 663'.62—dc22   2007003895

*Cherry Lake Publishing would like to acknowledge the work of
The Partnership for 21st Century Skills.
Please visit www.21stcenturyskills.org for more information.*

TABLE OF CONTENTS

CHAPTER ONE
A New Drink   4

CHAPTER TWO
Too Much Corn   8

CHAPTER THREE
As Sweet as Sugar   13

CHAPTER FOUR
How Cola Is Made   18

CHAPTER FIVE
From the Warehouse to the Store   22

Map   28

Glossary   30

For More Information   31

Index   32

About the Author   32

CHAPTER ONE

A New Drink

A woman selects fresh fish at a street market in Dakar, Senegal.

Julia and her parents arose early to go to the Sandaga Market. It was the largest market in Dakar, the capital of Senegal, a nation in West Africa. As they approached, the vivid colors of the market greeted and soon surrounded them. Long tables covered in gold, blue, scarlet, and green cloth stretched along the street. The women behind the tables wore bright outfits and matching headdresses. Multicolored umbrellas sprouted everywhere to keep the hot sun off the sellers and their customers.

Julia's parents led the way inside a stall. There Julia saw large crates of fish and boxes of vegetables. The smell of smoke from cooking grills was everywhere.

Her father pointed to a vendor who sat next to buckets of nuts bunched up and wrapped in plastic bags. "Those are kola nuts," her father said.

Hearing the word kola reminded Julia of her favorite drink. She felt thirsty. She had learned one thing about Senegal already: it was hot.

"What are kola nuts?" she asked.

"People here chew them for energy," her father said. "A long time ago, cola drinks contained a liquid taken from kola nuts. The nuts contain caffeine. That's a chemical that gives people a jolt of energy."

"Can we make cola out of them?" Julia asked. "Because I'd like something to drink."

"It takes a lot more than kola nuts to make cola," he said.

"I can help," Julia's mother said.

She took Julia's hand and led her down an aisle. Vendors called out in French, trying to get them to look at their products. The further they walked, the thirstier Julia felt. Finally, her mother knelt down.

"Take your pick," she said.

A man sat behind a table lined with cans. Julia recognized Coca-Cola and Pepsi cans.

"We can get soda from home here?" she asked in surprise.

"Yes," her mother said. "They're made in a lot of different countries. Here's some money. Just go up and point to the can you want."

In May 1886, John Stith Pemberton, a physician and chemist in Atlanta, Georgia, created a beverage based on the kola nut. Originally from Africa and brought to the Americas by slaves, the kola nut had a slightly bitter taste. What was most significant,

John Stith Pemberton (1831–1888) was a highly respected member of the medical profession in the state of Georgia.

however, was that it contained caffeine, an energy-boosting chemical also found in coffee, tea, and many of today's energy drinks. Pemberton's beverage was called Coca-Cola.

At first, Coca-Cola was sold as a sweet syrup to soda fountains in drug stores. There the syrup was mixed with **carbonated** water. The combination was so popular that the Coca-Cola Company began manufacturing its own fizzy cola.

Coca-Cola was not the first cola drink, but it was the first to have mass popularity. Rival colas sprang up all over the United States. From the 1930s on, Pepsi-Cola and Royal Crown (RC) Cola, among others, challenged Coca-Cola for customers.

Cola companies changed their recipes over the years, but sugar remained a basic ingredient. As the cost of sugar rose in the 1970s, companies looked for a less-expensive sweetener. One by one, they turned to a super-sweet substance taken from an unlikely source: corn.

21st Century Content

In 1893, pharmacist Caleb Bradham's homemade cola became popular in New Bern, North Carolina. Bradham's Pepsi-Cola grew into a successful company before running into money problems during World War I. Pepsi went out of business twice. In the 1930s, it returned with a new owner and a new headquarters in Long Island City, New York.

The reborn company used creative marketing methods. Pepsi charged a nickel for a 12-ounce (0.35-liter) bottle. Coke charged the same price for its 6.5-ounce (0.19-l) bottle. That kind of bargain was popular during the Great Depression, when millions of people were poor or unemployed, and Pepsi has prospered ever since.

CHAPTER TWO

Too Much Corn

Julia was so overcome with thirst that she grabbed the first Coca-Cola she could see. Her mom grabbed a Pepsi for herself, and her dad took an RC Cola. As Julia opened the top of the can she heard that old familiar fizz and took a cool, refreshing sip of her Coca-Cola.

"Hey dad, how is cola made?" asked Julia.

"Well, it's a very interesting process that goes through many different stages," Julia's dad explained.

"I'll explain it as we walk through the rest of the market. How is your Coca-Cola?" Julia's dad asked.

Corn fields cover about 80 million acres of U.S. farmland.

"Delicious!" exclaimed Julia.

Julia and her parents continued walking through the market, sipping their colas and looking at the goods offered by different vendors. Julia's dad went on to explain the complex process of how cola gets produced.

"Back in the United States the cola production process starts in the corn fields," Julia's dad explained. "And many of those corn fields can be found in states like Iowa, Illinois, and Nebraska."

"There's corn in cola?" Julia asked, surprised.

"Well, sort of. It's one of many ingredients that go into the production of cola. But the whole process starts with corn," Julia's dad emphasized.

The United States leads the world in corn production. In 2005–2006, the country produced 282,260,000 metric tons of corn, more than double second-place China's 139,365,000 metric tons. Corn grows on about 80 million acres of U.S. farmland, with Iowa, Illinois, and Nebraska the top-producing states. Farmers in the United States grow so much corn that some storage facilities have to pile the extra outdoors in heaps that can tower six stories high.

This is a problem because of the economic law of **supply and demand**. According to the law of supply and demand, the price of a product will go up if it becomes scarce (low supply) or if people want more than what's

*Ethanol, also known as ethyl alcohol, is a clear,
colorless liquid often made from corn.*

available (high demand). By the same rule, the price goes down if there is a large supply or if people do not want the amount that's available.

Those six-story-high piles of extra corn would drive down the price. Farmers often react to low prices by growing more corn. They have to sell more and more to make the same amount of money. Unfortunately, that adds to the problem because it means more excess corn. Under normal market conditions, such a glut drives the price of corn down.

But as it turns out, this only happens to a certain point. To prevent further loss to the corn producers, the government steps in to stabilize the price of corn by giving **subsidies** to farming families and farming corporations. By doing so, the government protects their livelihood.

In 2005, the U.S. government spent about $23 billion in subsidies for agriculture, the highest amount ever. There are different types of subsidies. One type of subsidy gives money to farmers when misfortune strikes. For example, government subsidies reimburse growers for money lost because of natural disasters such as hurricanes or floods.

Another kind of subsidy pays farmers to use environmentally friendly methods of growing crops. Still another form of subsidy supports production of ethanol, an alternative fuel made from corn. This helps corn farmers in two ways. First, ethanol makers use some of the excess corn. Second, getting rid of excess corn keeps corn prices higher and corn farmers happy.

Subsidies are not unusual. Most nations protect producers of one or more of its agricultural products.

Another common protective policy is a **tariff**, a tax on a product brought in from another country. For example, the U.S. government

Corn, also called maize, was one of the most important crops in ancient America. Experts generally accept that people in central Mexico began to cultivate an ancestor of modern maize in about 8000 B.C., ten thousand years ago. The plant was a cross between that ancestor and teosinte, a native grass with kernel-like seeds.

Maize farming spread from central Mexico. By the time Christopher Columbus arrived in the Americas in 1492, maize fed people from the Andes mountains to New England. This was not the sweet corn that we are used to eating today. How do you think the hard corn kernels were used back then?

places a fifty-four-cent tariff on every gallon of ethanol that comes from outside the country. Why? To make ethanol brought in from other countries too expensive to compete with ethanol made in the United States.

For many years, government programs such as subsidies and tariffs protected American sugar farmers in much the same way. But in the late 1970s, the system changed and sugar prices started to rise.

Cola manufacturers noticed. They bought tons of sugar to sweeten their drinks. Even a slight price increase would cost them millions of dollars. Soft drink companies looked around for an alternative sweetener.

One made from corn soon became less expensive than sugar. High fructose corn syrup (HFCS) changed people's tastes, the way cola was made, and even the most famous secret recipe in the world.

CHAPTER THREE

AS SWEET AS SUGAR

Cola is bottled in a manufacturing facility.

Julia listened to her father explain the whole corn production process, and began to realize what an important part corn plays in the production of cola.

"So the corn syrup that they produce from the corn harvested from the fields is what makes my Coca-Cola sweet?" Julia asked.

"Exactly!" Julia's dad answered. "They use the corn to produce something called high fructose corn syrup. HFCS is what is used to make your drink so sweet and tasty."

As Julia took another sip of her Coca-Cola, her father explained why corn was so important to the cola recipe.

Sugar from sugar cane plants was used to sweeten colas before high fructose corn syrup was created.

"They found that they could make cola sweet by using high fructose corn syrup instead of sugar. And HFCS costs less than sugar, too!"

"When did they start using corn syrup to sweeten colas?" Julia's mom asked.

"Yeah, and how do they make it, Dad?" also asked Julia.

Julia's dad went on to explain how cola companies started using corn syrup as Julia and her mom took another sip of their colas, savoring every last sweet, tasty drop!

Research into making sweeteners from corn began in the 1950s. In 1971, Yoshiyuki Takasaki, a scientist at the Japanese Fermentation Research Institute, took out a **patent** for the corn-based sweetener he created. It was known as high fructose corn syrup (HFCS). Several companies worked to improve high fructose corn syrup until, in 1972, it tasted as sweet as refined sugar. That opened the door for its use in foods and beverages.

By the late 1970s, Coca-Cola and Pepsi, the cola industry leaders, agreed to let HFCS be used in their juices and non-cola drinks. But the colas, the biggest sellers, presented a problem.

Coca-Cola had always guarded its recipe. Even today, it is stored in a vault deep within SunTrust bank in Atlanta. For a hundred years, people have wondered what goes into the company's famous secret formula.

Company leaders feared switching from sugar, Coke's usual sweetener, to HFCS. Doing so meant tampering with the drink's hugely successful taste.

It took years of testing, but Coca-Cola researchers matched the taste of HFCS in Coke to that of sugar. In 1980, the company okayed the use of HFCS in its cola.

Because Coca-Cola used the less-expensive HFCS, it saved an estimated $70 million in 1983. Pepsi switched to HFCS the next year.

Meanwhile, HFCS manufacturers expanded to handle the new, increased demand. Two companies soon emerged as the industry's leaders. Cargill, Inc., of Minneapolis, Minnesota, employs 149,000 people in more than sixty countries. The agricultural giant Archer Daniels Midland, headquartered in Decatur, Illinois, has operated since 1902. Both companies produce HFCS as one of their many food-related products.

Corn's transformation into HFCS begins with a technique called wet mill processing. Wet mill processing begins by soaking the corn kernels in water. Machinery then grinds down the wet corn. Other processes separate starch from unwanted parts of the corn, leaving behind a heavy liquid called a slurry.

The slurry goes into steel vats and undergoes a multistep process. Special bacteria and proteins cause chemical reactions to transform the slurry. Spinning the mixture at high speed separates out unwanted molecules. The result is a substance that is 90 percent fructose. Manufacturers then add glucose to make HFCS, and the final product is a thick, colorless liquid.

The formula is altered, depending on the product it is going into. The HFCS that sweetens cola is 55 percent fructose and 45 percent glucose. Less-sweet foods such as yogurt and white bread use a formula that's 42 percent fructose and 58 percent glucose.

21st Century Content

Cola lovers in the United States and Canada drink soft drinks made with high fructose corn syrup. Popular soft drink makers with manufacturing plants in some other nations, such as Brazil and Australia, though, still sweeten drinks with sugar. Those countries use tariffs and subsidies to keep the price of sugar lower than the price of HFCS. Many people claim they can taste the difference.

CHAPTER FOUR

How Cola Is Made

"Wow, I never knew how complicated it is to make a can of cola!" Julia exclaimed.

"Or how long HFCS has been part of the recipe," Julia's mother added.

"You're absolutely right, Julia. It's a long, complex process just to make the sweetener in cola, but there is still more to the process of making the whole drink," Julia's father added.

Julia, still amazed by the fact that there was corn in her soft drink, was wondering how the rest of the cola production process works.

"So Dad, how does the rest of the cola get made?" Julia asked.

Julia's dad went on to explain the rest of the cola production process.

Products from many parts of the world contribute to cola's pleasing taste. One of the ingredients in cola is vanilla. In ancient Mexico, the Totonac people farmed vanilla beans near the modern-day city of Papantla. In about 1870, the French recognized vanilla as a valuable product and planted it in their tropical colonies. The vanilla bean remains an important crop in those lands, including Madagascar (now an independent nation) and the nearby islands of Réunion and the Comoros, and Tahiti. Vanilla is still farmed in Mexico and also produced in Indonesia, India, and Papua New Guinea.

Another flavor, cinnamon, has been valuable for centuries. The ancient Egyptians used it in burial ceremonies. Several species of the *Cinnamomum* tree yield cinnamon. The best comes from Sri Lanka. A lot of today's cinnamon, including that used in the United States, comes from Southeast Asia's cassia tree, a species related to the *Cinnamomum*.

Vanilla beans are the seed pods of certain types of tropical orchid plants.

In cola, vanilla and cinnamon are often combined with citrus flavors. The nut that gave cola its name is rarely used anymore. Combinations of other flavors, and other sources of caffeine, have replaced the kola nut.

The major cola companies do not make the finished product that is sold on grocery store shelves. They manufacture the **concentrate**, which is the core of the cola's flavor. For a long time, the concentrate was made in the United States and shipped overseas. As soft drink companies have expanded into new countries, it's become necessary to have the concentrates made closer to

West African peoples have long used parts of the kola tree to treat ailments. The seeds, for instance, help with problems such as nausea and diarrhea. West Africans also dry and chew the 2-inch-long (5-centimeter-long) nut to boost energy.

The nut is also important in African culture. In parts of Senegal, a bridegroom is expected to offer a large bag of kola nuts to his future in-laws. The Igbo people of Nigeria consider the nut sacred and use it in religious ceremonies.

where the drink itself is created—at companies called bottlers. The Coca-Cola company, for instance, makes its concentrate in Shanghai, China, for its large chain of Chinese bottlers, and in Manaus, Brazil, for the Brazilian market.

The system of working through bottlers dates from the earliest days of the cola industry. Beverage companies gave a bottler a **franchise** that lasted as long as the bottler observed the terms of the contract with the supplier of the concentrate. When the franchise owner died, the franchise could be passed on to an heir. Bottling companies became family businesses.

The bottling plants complete the production process. Each bottler signs a contract to produce the finished beverage and package it in bottles and cans. Today, bottling is a high-speed, high-volume operation. A bottling plant can turn out more than two thousand soft drinks every minute.

The production process starts by combining purified water with either HFCS (in the United States) or refined sugar (elsewhere). Workers at the plant test the water to keep out bacteria and unwanted particles. Once the two ingredients are mixed together, the mixture is filtered again to get rid of any remaining impurities, just to be safe.

The sweetened water is then combined with the concentrate provided by the parent company. When a batch is ready, workers add carbonation to the water, to give the cola its bubbles. An approved batch is then ready for packaging.

Lines of bottles or cans move down a high-speed conveyor belt. Machines fill each container to the exact same level and cap it. Another conveyor belt sends the bottles to be labeled. Aluminum cans come with the brand name and other information already on them.

Machinery packs the containers into shipping cartons. Workers haul the cartons to the bottler's warehouse, where the cola awaits shipment to the public.

21st Century Content

While American companies dominate the cola industry in many nations, there are successful local brands. One of them is Big Cola, a Latin American company.

Chemist Carlos Añaños invented a drink called Kola Real and started a company in his native Peru. Soon the beverage spread to neighboring countries. In 2002, he set up a bottling plant in Puebla, east of Mexico City, and released a version of his drink called Big Cola.

In two years, Big Cola had taken 5 percent of Mexico's cola market away from the American brands. The company had borrowed a lesson from history. It sold more of its product at a cheaper price—just as Pepsi once sold a bigger bottle of soda for a nickel to compete with Coca-Cola.

CHAPTER FIVE

FROM THE WAREHOUSE TO THE STORE

Colas are not the only soft drinks sweetened with high fructose corn syrup.

Julia tried to understand everything her father had just told her about how cola is made.

"So cola ingredients are gathered from all over the world?" Julia asked.

"That's right! Whether it's vanilla from Mexico, corn from the United States, or cinnamon from Sri Lanka, many people all over the world play a part in producing cola," Julia's dad explained.

"Since all these people help out with making the colas, shouldn't they get colas too?" Julia's mom asked.

"They definitely should!" suggested Julia.

"And they most certainly do," explained Julia's dad. "How do you think you are able to drink that cola in your hand now, here in West Africa?"

Julia, almost through with her cola, was eager to learn more about how cola gets distributed throughout the world. Her dad went on to explain this process, too.

The franchise arrangement between soft drink companies and bottlers guarantees the bottler control of **distribution** in a geographic area. This goes back to the industry's early days. If a bottler manufactured Royal Crown Cola, for example, no other Royal Crown bottler could sell the drink in his territory.

The family-owned bottlers that dominated in the early years are hard to find today. Since the 1980s, large corporations have bought smaller bottlers and control a wide range of territories.

The largest bottling company is Coca-Cola Enterprises, called CCE on the stock market. Owned in part by the Coca-Cola Company (maker of the soft drinks), CCE is the largest soft drink distributor in the world. CCE's 73,000 workers make and distribute Coca-Cola products in 46 states, Canada, and in European countries such as France and Great Britain. Another manufacturing and distribution giant is the Pepsi Bottling Group, or PBG. Its 100 factories employ about 67,000 people. Thanks to the large number of bottling plants, a shipment of cola seldom has to travel far from the warehouse to the grocery stores, gas stations, restaurants, vending machine operators, and other businesses that stock the beverage.

Most colas are delivered to stores by trucks that service a particular area, or route.

In the United States, trucks do a majority of the transporting. Each driver has a list of locations, called a route, to make his or her deliveries. A driver in a large city may make deliveries within a small geographic area because there are so many stores and other businesses that carry the cola. In a rural area such as Wyoming, however, the opposite is true. Long-distance semis may haul the cola to local warehouses, where it is stored until it is delivered to individual businesses.

The distribution system has allowed cola companies to serve customers in all but the most remote parts of the world. Companies in many nations can only dream of distributing their product so widely. Still, problems arise. Even Coca-Cola, a brand available in 200 countries, has to deal with issues. Many concern bottlers. Since the bottlers are local companies, they sometimes get mixed up in local problems.

In many nations, it benefits a company to give business to officials, relatives of important leaders, or other people connected to power. That way, those in charge make money. For example, to set up business in the Central Asian country of Uzbekistan, Coca-Cola gave the major bottling franchise to the Uzbek dictator's son-in-law. It was later alleged the bottler hid millions of dollars from both Uzbekistan's government and the Coca-Cola Company. The son-in-law got in trouble, and the case hurt Coca-Cola's image.

And there have been other problems. **Pesticides** were found in beverages in India. Bottlers in Colombia were accused of hiring thugs to harass—even kill—people in labor unions. While these kinds of issues mostly concern local bottlers, the negative press reports stick to the parent company and sometimes become controversial in the United States. Managing these controversies is one more aspect of doing business in the global marketplace.

The unique cursive letters spelling out Coca-Cola and the familiar red, white, and blue Pepsi label are symbols of the global economy. Just as cola is popular around the world, it wouldn't exist without products from many countries. The vanilla comes from Mexico and Madagascar, the cinnamon from Southeast Asia, and the corn in HFCS from farms in Illinois, Iowa, and Nebraska.

Cola truly belongs to the world.

Julia heard the slurp at the end of her straw, and with one last sip she finished her cola.

"That was delicious!" exclaimed Julia.

"Mine was great too!" added Julia's mom.

"Wow, I never knew how complicated it was to make cola. And the best part is that we can get it anywhere in the world!" Julia exclaimed.

"Of course. As long as people keep producing the ingredients and manufacturers keep producing it, there will always be plenty of delicious, sweet-tasting cola for everyone." explained Julia's dad.

A Japanese girl in a traditional kimono sips a cola.

"So Mom, which is better, Coca-Cola or Pepsi?" asked Julia shyly.

Julia's parents laughed together as her mom answered.

"That, Julia, is a question for the ages!"

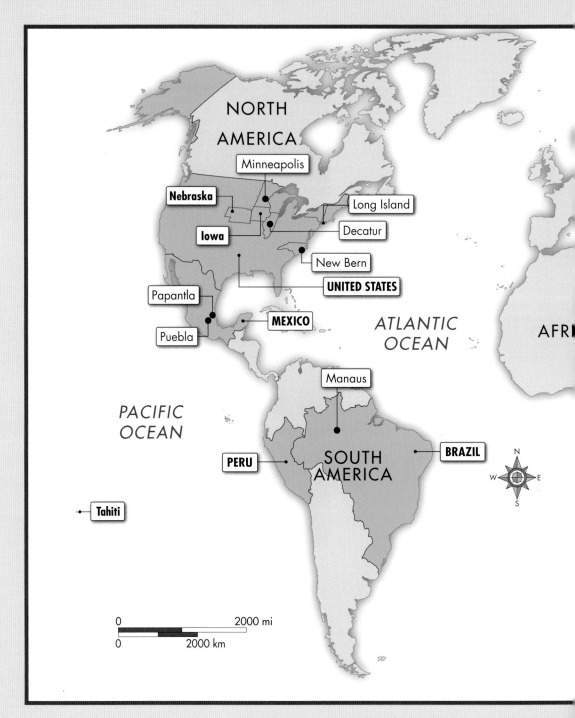

This map shows the countries and cities mentioned in the text.

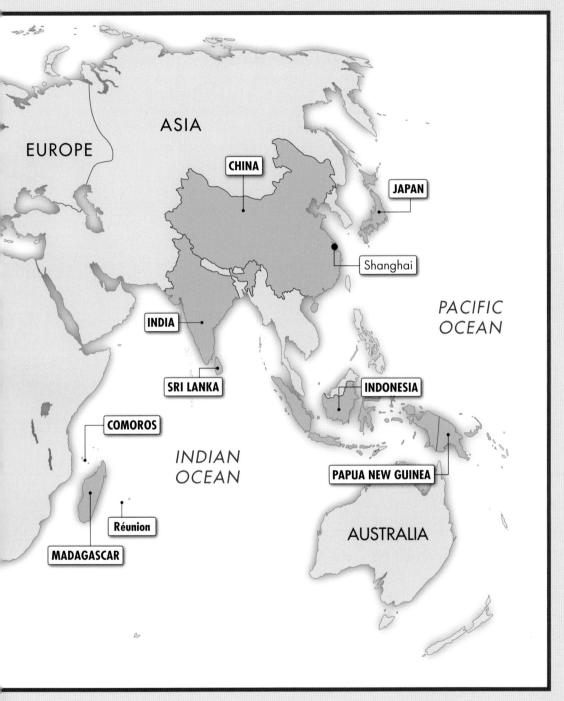

ASIA

EUROPE

CHINA

JAPAN

Shanghai

INDIA

PACIFIC
OCEAN

SRI LANKA

INDONESIA

COMOROS

PAPUA NEW GUINEA

INDIAN
OCEAN

Réunion

MADAGASCAR

AUSTRALIA

...hey are the locations of some of the companies involved in the making and selling of colas.

Glossary

carbonated (KAR-bun-ate-ed) Something that is carbonated has been combined with carbon dioxide. Carbonated water has many small bubbles in it.

concentrate (KON-sun-trayt) A concentrate is a thick, strongly flavored liquid. Colas are made by adding water to a cola-flavored concentrate.

distribution (diss-tri-BYOO-shuhn) Distribution is the system used by businesses to get products from where they are manufactured to various places where they will be sold.

franchise (FRAN-chize) A franchise is an agreement with a person or group allowing them to distribute and sell a corporation's products in a particular geographic area.

patent (PAT-uhnt) A patent is the legal document giving an inventor the sole rights to manufacture and sell his or her invention.

pesticides (PESS-tuh-sidez) Pesticides are chemicals used to kill insects and other pests.

subsidies (SUHB-suh-deez) In agriculture, subsidies are government payments to encourage farmers to run their operations in certain ways or to compensate for losses because of misfortunes such as natural or man-made disasters.

supply and demand (suh-PLY and di-MAND) The economic law of supply and demand states that the price of a good depends on how much of a good is available (supply) and how much of a good is wanted by customers (demand).

tariff (TARE-iff) A tariff is a tax on a product brought in from another country.

FOR MORE INFORMATION

Books

Bell, Lonnie. *The Story of Coca-Cola*. Mankato, MN: Smart Apple Media, 2003.

Karner, Julie. *The Biography of Vanilla*. New York: Crabtree Publishing, 2006.

Landau, Elaine. *American Icons: Nike, McDonalds, Coca-Cola, Levi Strauss*. Brookfield, CT: Twenty-First Century Books, 2003.

Web Sites

The Coca-Cola Company: The Chronicle of Coca-Cola
www2.coca-cola.com/heritage/chronicle_birth_refreshing_idea.html
The history of Coca-Cola

Pepsi USA: Ads and History
www.pepsi.com/help/faqs/faq.php?category=ads_and_history&page=highlights
A history of Pepsi advertising

RC Cola: Royal Crown Then and Now
www.rccolainternational.com/then/flash.html
A timeline of Royal Crown's history with pictures

INDEX

Añaños, Carlos, 21
Archer Daniels Midland, 16
Atlanta, Georgia, 6, 15

Big Cola, 21
bottling companies, 20–21,
    23–26
Bradham, Caleb, 7

caffeine, 5, 7, 19
calories, 16
carbonation, 7, 21
Cargill, Inc., 16
cinnamon, 19, 22, 26
citrus flavors, 19
Coca-Cola, 5, 7, 8, 13,–16,
    20, 21, 23, 25–27
Coca-Cola Enterprises (CCE), 23
Columbus, Georgia, 6
concentrate, 19–21
corn, 7–15, 17, 18, 22, 26

Dakar, Senegal, 4
Decatur, Illinois, 16
delivery routes, 25
Diet Rite, 6
distribution, 23–25

ethanol, 10–12

franchises, 20, 23, 25
fructose, 12, 14, 15, 17, 22

glucose, 17
Great Depression, 7

high fructose corn syrup (HFCS),
    12–18, 20–21, 26

Japanese Fermentation Research
    Institute, 15

kola nuts, 5, 6–7, 19, 20
Kola Real, 21

Long Island City, New York, 7

Manaus, Brazil, 20
marketing, 7
Minneapolis, Minnesota, 16

New Bern, North Carolina, 7

patents, 15
Pemberton, John Stith, 6, 7
Pepsi Bottling Group (PBG), 24
Pepsi Cola, 5, 7, 8, 15, 16,
    21, 24, 26, 27

pesticides, 26
production process, 9, 13,
    17–21

recipes, 12, 14, 15–16, 18
Royal Crown (RC) Cola, 6, 7,
    8, 23

Sandaga Market, 4
Shanghai, China, 20
shipping, 19, 21, 24
slurry, 17
subsidies, 11, 12, 17
sugar, 6, 7, 12–17, 21
sugar-free cola, 6
SunTrust bank, 15
supply and demand, 9–10

Takasaki, Yoshiyuki, 15
tariffs, 11–12, 17
teosinte, 12

Uzbekistan, 25

vanilla, 18, 19, 22, 26

Web sites, 16
wet mill processing, 17
World War I, 7

ABOUT THE AUTHOR

Kevin Cunningham is the author of several books, including biographies of Joseph Stalin and J. Edgar Hoover and a series on diseases in human history. He lives in Chicago.